The Phoenix Living Poets

WHEN THE WORDS
ARE GONE

WHEN THE WORDS ARE GONE

by

HARDIMAN SCOTT

CHATTO AND WINDUS

THE HOGARTH PRESS

1972

Published by
Chatto and Windus Ltd
with The Hogarth Press Ltd
42 William IV Street
London W.C.2

★

Clarke, Irwin & Co. Ltd
Toronto

ISBN 0 7011 1914 4

© Hardiman Scott 1972

Printed in Great Britain

CONTENTS

For John and for Sue

Landscape, Boxford, Suffolk

Above the village the ploughed ridges slope –
Brown earth air-softened as thrushes feathers –
To a deckle of trees sewing a seam
Between fields, and drawing a line to mark
The underlying shape settled ages
Before these cultivations. Winter wheat shows
Its early green, and on clear days, in these
First months, there's a pastel light that shades where
Landscape folds fawn against blue, and distance
Sharpens the half-perceived familiar things.

The air makes moving invisible moulds
Over everywhere, slips through the furrows
And off the sides of saplings, and shivers
Through the green and tentative, pointing wheat;
And branches move within limits imposed
By growth. Birds court the currents, create, part
Them with briefly seen intentions. Hornpies
Especially carving aerobatic
Fretworks in flight. So always there is this
Imposition of ever-changing shapes.

These patterns, unseen, half-seen, have a kind
Of familiarity, or perhaps
A certainty contained by the land's fall;
Its own first shape that alone is seen, stays
Beneath the air-shapes, growth, and all that moves.
And standing here I would project on air
My own invisible cast among all
The others that have looked or worked, so this
Transience might become of the patterns,
A kind of ghost to be sensed on this land.

Suffolk Lane

All night it has rained:
Sound of stippling constantly on the tiles,
Scrabbling of sheltering birds under eaves,
Water poised like pained
Breath before it slips from the oversail
And pads on to the last of winter's leaves.

This morning I walk
Slowly up the lane where the land rises
Towards Horner's Green. The sky is washed blue.
Sunlight grows straw stalks
Out of pebbles, and last night's rain rushes
With the chortling of blackbird warnings through

Mud gullies and grass
At the lane's edge. Air is soft with herbage
And winter-pressed leaves, as though two seasons
Distil where they pass
The scent of all their mornings and make fresh
The fields and lane where last night's water runs.

Where end-of-year green
Straight sticks lean open from the hedge, I see
The fringe of woods and the draggled quarters
Where the rooks have been,
And the swell of river where sunlight skis
Unseen shoes of wind across the waters.

And all this I know,
As though childhood had owned these lands and now
Returned them, giving meaning to this lane
And to me. Although
Not to make too much of this, as I turn
I feel at last I have come home again.

Dedham Mill

by JOHN CONSTABLE

Some object is always needed
To point the experience,
To translate it, perhaps transmute it,
For when everything has yielded
The chance elements, the sense
Only comes with the permanence
That we alone make of it.

So the mill, reflecting its brown age
In the pond, russeting with an autumn
The trees cosset before they've done
With summer, stills the rage
That worries your sky, and gives some
Reason not for paint, but living,
When life is almost falling.

The church means nothing here.
The trees sustain a balance
When the seasons alone compel,
And the single element of fear
Is in the light, and the chance
Arrangement of clouds,
Revealing only your own will.

And the clouds had changed almost
Before you'd begun. So we need
The mill, not for meaning's sake
Or the purpose you have imposed,
But as symbol and as shelter,
A place we have made against the need
For love, and autumn, and heartbreak.

Morning After Snow

When we woke the willow
Was a lattice of white
Cottons stitched to the cold morning,
Till the sun rising low
Turned the threads to silky light
And left the trellised snow trembling.

All night it had fallen,
Spreading its polar fur
Across the fields, leaving flashes
Down trees, and had written
A scribbling on twigs where
They stood stark in the winds' leashes.

Walking up the lane we
Plunged in the foam of it
And saw where it fluttered like lace
On hog-weed heads and tree
Tips distantly and, lit
By sun, shimmered as wind-freshed fleece.

The fields rolled whitely round
Smooth billows, sharp against
A blue so cold and intense that
It seemed like the high sound
Of strings, and then we sensed
In crystal air almost a thought

Of movement and, turning,
Saw a single pheasant,
A dun hen flying near the stream's
Edge, and this thrash of wings,
This other life aslant,
Like our own, the landscape's fall, seemed

Amid the snow's strangeness,
To make all known again,
And we became aware of forms
Hidden, and so felt less
Unsure that, in this lane,
We know, are known for what we are.

Henry Tooley of Ipswich

died 1551

A brass, an almshouse, sundry documents,
And an account book, two-thirds full, closely
Written with the cryptic tales of trading –
The tuns of wine, the cloths sent out to Spain
And the outfitting of ships for Iceland
Fishing, the entries crossed over as debts
Were settled – these are the remaining bits
Of evidence that establish your wealth,
Your importance in the ways of the town.

Much more we have to infer. For instance,
That you were a self-made man, testing faith
With a native care against advantage.
So you were a man strong enough to take
The tide, to ride it through the fast-changing
Currents of your time; and tough enough to
Turn the winds to your own fortune; and true
Enough to your will to hunt a quarry
Through the Courts and make the law your purpose.

Against the virtue of these qualities,
Then, you might have been stubborn, easily pushed
To anger and not always just. How else
Explain why you sent that poor sheepshearer –
George Banes was his name – in and out of gaol
For no apparent reason, or how you
Briefly were made a stranger of your own town
For not accepting justice done to you?
Still, you got your fine reduced. Clever too.

But a thoughtful host no doubt, not mincing
Words to your wife to get rid of workmen
About the house, "jonnars and the massons",
Because guests were coming. And generous
In death, remembering the disabled,
The poor, and making homes for them; a gift
To fatherless maids on their wedding day –
That perhaps the one shy tribute to love,
The hint of other evidence, unfound.

Yet there's always the historical view:
You, symbol of changing society;
The rise of the trading classes, while men
Burned for their beliefs, lands changed hands, and the
Economy changed men. But I would look
For more than this, more than accounts confess,
For some identity of then and now,
In thought, care, or love, that would give sense to
"Whose affayres God furtherid with successe."

Mary Queen of Scots at work on the tapestries at Tutbury Castle

My conscience, no doubt, could "find a humbler place",
But could my hands a humbler employment find?
It would be tedious were it not for
The gay diversity of the colours
That give my wits leave to sharpen idleness
With thoughts like arrows finding their own target
In some future state; thoughts of what might yet be,
What, pray God, could have been once, less humbly,
Had not my love crossed their lords, and my blood,
Its passion, its pride, its royalty too,
Angered them with godly jealousies of me.

"To love and serve" him loyally – that was my wish,
With my unsad guilt so soon upon him,
For what a worthy guilt is the guilt of love.
But they mistake me if they think I'm held
By castle walls and not my own conviction.
I trade rather than lose my liberty,
Working these silks by the hour until pain
Makes me to give over.

        See now, I've woven
A hand through a cloud to clasp a sickle
And prune the vines – a reminder, I say,
That virtue is strengthened by wounds;
Which I should know as well as any,
For I sent Norfolk the same upon a cushion.
Not that I think of him. Necessity
Could bring him to my bed, but how cold I should lie.
Although, he takes to his purpose well – except
They need not think I shall be a Spanish puppet.
My pride is too pure for that;
There is too much I owe my blood.

Look! – this pheasant. His bronze tail is far too long.
The panel won't contain it. It shall be cut short,
And the rest I'll embroider above his back.
It begins to look well, I think. That leopard
Has a saucy look. And this solemn bird
With a thick hatchet for a beak – how curious.
And the dolphin – how I like the way he arches
In a blue wave. Yes, it begins to look well.

There's a pleasure in such things, a humour too,
And the silks prettily disguise my sorrow;
As they give patience to my love to bear
"Pain and dishonour in a life unsure."

Oh God, in those words I think of him again
To whom they tokened love, and made murder easy.
Now a fear that's not our own lies between us;
But as I can love, so can I hate, as fast,
As strong as this fingered steel and as bright;
Yes, as sharp as this plying needle-point
That would decieve me stitching these quiet fancies.
But the seams of State shall not be so well stitched
That an intriguing Time won't unpick them.
And Time can serve me if I judge it well.
If not, then this much I leave of beauty,
Out of my sorrow this much to delight.

Note—These tapestries have become known as the Oxburgh
Hangings, and are at Oxburgh Hall in Norfolk.

Robert Stephen Hawker's Hut, Morwenstow

Curiosity perhaps, scarcely more
Than a lazy wish to see the relics
Of your solitude, who so piously
Could deceive with your mermaid pranks at Bude;
And perhaps to catch a clue to presence
In the sea-diminished silence, no more
Than a wing's flicker off the rock-sheared shore.

So we took the path by the church, over
The stile of slate, as hard blue as the sea
With the bloom of dusk upon it, and through
The field, with the slow-nibbling sheep scattered
On black-stilted feet, to Vicarage Cliff
And red-streaked Henna, stone-stranded hair held
Ragged against the combing winds and sea.

There was an old stone roller like a wave
Breaking in the grasses, and the vicar,
His wife and daughter had come to this high
Edge between earth and sky, waiting the known
Familiar changes, the odd visitors.
"Are you looking for Hawker's hut?" he said.
"It's down by the right path, at the cliff's head."

He'd never found the well St Morwenna
Used, sunk by a nameless path in the rocks;
So we remarked politely the Norman
Door of his church – your church so expressly
Cared for – these marks and remnants of others,
The sum that we call history, imprints
Of your devotions, quite invisible.

The hut we almost missed – the tangled grass
Roofing it; cut back, hollowed in the cliff,
Lined with stone and seal-bloomed slate, with narrow
Seat, also of slate, and a stable door.
We could only crouch inside and look out
At the silk-breathing, distant-rustled sea
And Sharpnose Point, hard, grey, upward shelving.

Here you carved well your niche of solitude,
A hard but a simple psalming of hands
That knew what they were about, building stone
Or pointing verse – much the same in the end,
Just as you built a double edifice of marriage,
A double truth of faith, going to Rome
On your death bed. So you had it both ways.

Such an incongruous and still silence,
We could not hear "the music of their wing",
Neither the air-slipped gulls nor your own near
Imagined "Angels of the spring", and yet
Easy to believe their ministering.
But for you there was movement in silence,
And finding these stirrings you asked no more.

Suffolk House (I)

How sometimes a place, a house, decides,
No matter what our preconceptions,
What we thought, what we wanted, it rides
Over with its own soft assertions.

This house, for example, built I'd say
For the cottager's shuttle, when lands
Rising from Box and Brett were astray
With sheep; built by the first Tudor hands,

This was not what we wanted at all.
Hard on the lane's edge, without a view,
Held close by others, backed by a wall,
It spoke against all we thought we knew.

What was it then that hot afternoon
In the stud-framed coolness of the room
Decided this near-five-hundredth June
Would mark the start of another home?

We scarcely had any say in it.
We were being accepted as two
More of the numberless tenants fit
To see a bit of history through.

What coming together could this be,
And who or what was judged and judging?
Were we heirs to memories, quickly
Touched within the wood ourselves touching?

Hard to believe we were the crux of
Histories, lives that every beam hides;
And yet coming to this point in love,
How strange it is that a house decides.

Suffolk House (II)

I hear the timbers knock in this old house,
Cold and empty but for us
Lying in this rib-cage of oak
And night folded about in moon laves. Truss
Upon truss of shadow strokes
Across my eyes sea-waves of gentle fear,
As I hear timbers knock in this old house.

I think ghosts seized my dreams in this old house,
Shook me silently from sleep,
So that I think of the dead
And am reminded how little we keep
Of all that was lived and said,
Loved and made to last. Wattle and plaster
Make ghosts that seize my dreams in this old house.

Night harbours the lost hosts in this old house,
The forgotten acts that gave
Life meaning and some belief
And taught of love a tenderness to save
Against the night's sobbing grief;
But neither I awake nor you asleep
Can harbour the lost hosts in this old house.

So we shall not be new in this old house.
It will take time to assuage
Each host the imprinted past,
And make a home that adds a touch of age
Before it's lost to the last.
Care and love – we must use them both, or else
We never shall be known in this old house.

Suffolk House (III)

The shape of the house is still here
Just as it was laid down on the earth
Nearly five hundred years ago:
A rectangle of oak that now,
Ridged and lined, crinkled like old skin
Or the far sight of a ploughed field
From the air, still makes your plan clear:
Simply to build a shelter here.

But what is left tells us nothing
Of your purpose: perhaps a home,
A place for spinners or weavers,
Merely a store for bales of wool.
Yet what centuries have changed leaves
Unaltered the first intentions
Of your hands: not, you'd say, profound,
Just to sign your craft on the ground.

There was bread to work for. Perhaps
A wife and children had some claim
Upon your skill and carpentry.
And the times, I should like to think,
Turned from those late, too common deaths
Some favours to your hands, and thus
This unexpected endurance
Of your days' work stands upon chance.

Necessity does not always
Live this long, but I suspect you
Would not want these beetle-peppered
Timbers hard with age to do more
Than stand as symbols of your craft.
I should like these lines to stand half
As well to mark where time dovetails
Our unknown lives and common love.

Two Poems for Sue

I

Nothing will remain

Knowledge that knows no other word than love
Can't be sculpted from stone or cast in bronze,
Or noted below the line or above,
Between the staves, to be studied by dons,
Performed and praised in this and any age;
Or painted, every stroke of brush or knife
Like lines in a poem printing a page,
Making immortal one segment of life.

But of all our love nothing will remain.
It cannot be looked at or read or played.
Living it is no statue to contain
The immortalities that art has made.
No-one will ever know or can devise
The scent and colour of the rose that dies.

II

Return to a Room

It was such a day as this,
Because I remember the light
Through your eyelashes, fanning
An aura of gold, slight
And shadowy, on your cheeks,
As you lay in the chair, spanning
With your hands' touch weeks
Of longing for such a day as this.

Now after eleven years,
To come back and find the room
Just the same – the Corot prints,
You, aged twelve, the bloom
Of rose-lighted windows
Scattering on tables their tints
Like petals the wind blows
With scents of eleven known years.

Where are we as once we were?
What this room gave and we've taken
And perfected, now that we're older
Do we meet younger and awaken
What was here, so the very air
Is ghostly with memories we stir?
But something added is also here
To make of us more than what we were.

Winds' Victories

We filled the house with the winds' victories.
Down the land, rattling into the village
Out of the east, searing the garden wall,
They seethed a flame and scythed across the earth.

The bare branches of the poplars bristled,
But the willow laid its long tresses out,
Flowing to the combing east, and willing
This rout of airs to make for longer growth.

But hyacinths and daffodils were snapped
And pinned in brilliant fretlings on the ground,
Crying out against this din with the crush
Of scent tattered to fragments on the wind.

So we gathered them up, took them indoors,
And filled every vase in the house, to heal
Their silent torment with water and hands'
Tenderness of touch and soft inquiry.

There may be more to it than this: colour
And scent filling interior spaces;
So that I wonder whether the flowers
Or we fill the house with the winds' victories.

Landscape near Sea Palling, Norfolk

Clenched fists of grubby willows
  Tune the sea-torn wind through stopped
    Trebles, stalked by the dykes, by acres
      Of grasses frowning their green-grey shallows.

Only the dunes marram-tight
  Against the wind's craft and the sea's
    Bite give height under the wide clouds
      Where gulls chip down their feathered light.

And the rusty brick cone of a mill,
  Its slatted sails crossed like arms
    Over a still-dead breast, blind
      Witness of this solitude, is dead and still.

The sea-torn wind cuts like a knife
  Truth in its slatting, so its crucifixion
    Nails against the sky the height
      And form of this land's lonely life.

Adlestrop

(To the memory of Edward Thomas)

Yes. I remember Adlestrop,
For I, too, was at Adlestrop
The other day – one afternoon
Early in July; not to stop

More than an hour or two, but long
Enough, it seemed, to meet with you
In and out of Time. There the station
Where your train had stopped, and a few

Young shorthorns grazing by the line,
The sunlight rusty on their flanks,
And willows; hay was done of course,
But meadowsweet was there, and banks

Of willow-herb like pink feathers
In the grass, and a blackbird – two
In fact, came chinking across the road
And vanished where brambles overgrew.

I found where the road twisted sharp
Into the village of Cotswold
Homes, and went into the little
Cottage post-office to be told

My way, but no-one was there. I'd
Come to see a farmer who'd been
Five years under these hills, but all
Was still in Adlestrop, and green

The tilting fields, and quiet too.
So that I wondered if your stop
And mine could have added meaning to
The singing birds in Adlestrop.

A Kind of Creation

I created Slade, that much I know.
He would have been nothing without me.
He owed me everything;
So I had to kill him.
Hardly a day passed but I killed him;
Hardly a day but he rose from the dead.

I sought him in the unexplored lands
Of the earth, riding a cycle through
The trees and sliding sand
Of Middleton woods, and
Always, thrust through the jungle creeper
And past the hissing snake, I was first.

In sandpits abandoned by workmen
On Saturday afternoons, hurtling
Fast along the rails
In clattering trucks,
Swooping to pit bottom, I outdared
And outraced him and left him beaten.

And in my pedal car on pavements
My roaring Bentley forced him over
The top at Brooklands.
From the conning tower
Of felled trunk and submarine I sought him
And shot him out of the green-grass waters.

Splendid I was with my rapier –
Cane poked through a piece of motor tyre –
Raiding hedgerow and ditch,
Startling sparrow and wren,
Flighting him full length to the gully,
Where he could choose my steel or the dyke.

I can't remember his final death,
Or if he escaped through some crevice
Of childish compassion;
But I wonder now less
At this memory, or his mission,
Than how I rose from the rising dead.

Two Poems in Memory of my Father

I

Elegy

The images were there,
The cornflower, the children playing,
The sounds in the street, where
Living and the fact of dying
Were as distant as a foreign war,
The commonplace as common as before.

The feeling was there too,
The incongruity, the loss,
Knowing there was nothing I could do
To temper absence, or to cross
The age of years and then to claim
The origins of love were still the same.

Then why was I afraid?
Was it fear halted the words,
Left the paper white, made
The meaning break like shards
That never could be formed to shape again?
Or grief perhaps that left the paper plain?

II

The Garden

The garden was like a memory of itself
    Bedraggled into old age.
    Enough of what I had known
Was left to recognize the features that the stealth
    Of years had marked with image
    On image of childhood, grown
Confused by those distant memories of itself.

Everything, for example, seemed so much smaller.
  But everything was there too –
  The paving stones cracked open
By roots and lichen, the pear tree gnarled and taller
  Than the crumbling wall it clung to,
  The rockery fallen, then
The grass, long, and strangling your conception smaller.

The pond was full of earth trailing tendrils of weed –
  Grave of an earlier death
  I remember one winter,
The rabbit prints on the snow left for me to read,
  As though through crystal, smeared breath
  Of ice disguising water,
And beneath, the silver shape in the swimming weed.

Now it is all overgrown, drab and neglected,
  Your loving of little worth.
  It might have been better changed,
So I didn't know all that age had rejected.
  It's the saddest part of birth
  That beauty becomes deranged.
The years fall like leaves on the garden neglected.

Polyanthus

You may seem, your round-eyed
Innocence opened wide,
An iris of yellow
And rose, damson and pink,
Fit flowers for a child,
Untouched by thoughtful hours.

But a child would not know
What age it takes to grow
This seeming innocence,
Or know this attribute
Is ours because we think,
Not because we're flowers.

It is not knowing you,
The mutual time that grew
Through our separate ways
To poems and petals
And sight in eyes that see
Single pupils of light.

Now thinking will not do,
Seeing does not see through
This too complex colour
For a child, too simple
Shape for us. Only scent
Distils what first was meant.

Escape

All our life, it seems, we're running away,
But what from is not altogether clear.
Perhaps it is the fact of not knowing
That is the ghost that meets our inward stare.

The stone is hard upon our knees at prayer;
The edifice of belief shakes, and light
Trembles at the feet of the crucifix,
And visions confuse our anxious sight.

All the philosophies that we invent,
The Socratic argument, and his door
Never to be opened lest we escape –
All these are the riches that make us poor.

Think of the patterns of apprehension
That some paintings have, how suddenly strike
The similarities we recognize
But do not know, and yet perceive we like.

Always it has been like this, and we crouch
By our streams, prospectors panning for gold,
At best shaking away a little dross,
Thinking we're young, not wanting to be old.

And love, even love, do we create this
Against all else? Is this our final say?
Our answer to not knowing why it is
We always seem to be running away?

When the words are gone

Now that summer has burned to tinder
And the sunlight turned yellow and cold on
The stripling trees, see how the leaves shale, shake
And fall, cut by the air's cold frieze, cut clean
They drift and fall, drift and float as frosty
Winds carry them curling down the sky, cast
Into the timeless indifference of space.

They are like words these leaves, some of them cut
Clean and sharp, geometric shapes of meaning;
Others rough and ragged like the freckle
Of ambiguity that complexions words.
And like words spoken into space they go,
Creating worlds briefly but endlessly,
Till at last they fall unheard upon the earth.

When all have fallen, gone their tattered ways
Into space, the tree limned naked and taut
In the cold air, stays; the summer's clothing
Shed, unsheathed it stands. And with words also,
The leaves of breath; for leaves nor words reveal
The tree. Only when the words are gone, cast
Into space, the poem, limned naked, stays.